RAILWAY POSTERS

Lorna Frost

SHIRE PUBLICATIONS

Published in Great Britain in 2013 by Shire Publications Ltd,
PO Box 883, Oxford OX1 9PL, United Kingdom.
PO Box 3985, New York, NY 10185-3983, USA.

E-mail: shire@shirebooks.co.uk   www.shirebooks.co.uk

A CIP catalogue record for this book is available from the
British Library.

Shire Library no. 658.   ISBN-13: 978 0 74781 084 1

Lorna Frost has asserted her right under the Copyright,
Designs and Patents Act, 1988, to be identified as the
author of this book.

Designed by Tony Truscott Designs, Sussex, UK
and typeset in Perpetua and Gill Sans.

Printed in China through Worldprint Ltd.

13 14 15 16 17   12 11 10 9 8 7 6 5 4 3

COVER IMAGE
A London & North Eastern Railway poster, 'Whitley Bay by
LNER', by Tom Purvis, *c.* 1935, part of the 'It's Quicker by
Rail' series.

TITLE PAGE IMAGE
'South for Winter Sunshine' by Edmond Vaughan, 1929,
was described by the *Railway Gazette* as 'curious', but its
striking modern composition is very effective.

CONTENTS PAGE IMAGE
The original painting for the London Midland & Scottish
Railway poster 'London by LMS, Piccadilly Circus by
Night', 1926, by Maurice Greiffenhagen RA.

ACKNOWLEDGEMENTS
My thanks to Ed Bartholomew, Ellen Tait, Matt Thompson
and my colleagues at the National Railway Museum for
their assistance.

All images are reproduced courtesy of the National
Railway Museum / Science and Society Picture Library.

THE NATIONAL RAILWAY MUSEUM
The National Railway Museum (NRM), York is the largest
railway museum in the world. Its permanent displays and
collections illustrate over 300 years of British railway
history, from the Industrial Revolution to the present day.
The NRM archive also includes a fabulous collection of
railway advertising posters charting the history of rail. Visit
www.nrm.org.uk to find out more.

This book is produced under licence from National
Museum of Science and Industry Trading Limited.
Royalties from the sale of this book help fund the National
Railway Museum's exhibitions and programmes. The
National Railway Museum Collection is a registered
trademark, no. 2309517.

Shire Publications is supporting the Woodland Trust, the UK's leading woodland conservation charity, by funding the dedication of trees.

CONTENTS

THE ESTABLISHMENT OF RAILWAY ADVERTISING

R AILWAY POSTERS have an enduring appeal that captures the imagination. They carry us off to faraway places of stunning landscapes and sandy beaches. They tell a story of luxurious travel, stylish couples and happy families. Railway posters throughout their history sell us a fantasy that we all want to believe in, but they also tell us something about the social, cultural and industrial developments of their time. The geographical expansion of the railways is shown in elaborate maps. Their architectural feats are beautifully and intricately observed in order to show their advancing infrastructure and facilities. A new-found freedom to travel, the emergence of the leisure industry, and the railways' influence on the growth of towns and resorts all over the United Kingdom are all evident in the imagery of the poster. Railway companies encouraged city breaks and travel abroad as well as in Britain; they advertised their own shipping and air services and published stylish images of modern locomotives designed to compete with increasing road traffic.

The birth of the railway poster was, however, somewhat less glamorous. It began with simple typeset notices and handbills, and it took almost to the end of the nineteenth century for railway poster advertising to make any real advancement in style.

The first advertising notices were produced in the 1820s and 1830s to herald the opening of new passenger railways across Britain. From the opening of the Stockton & Darlington Railway in 1825, letterpress notices were produced to announce the establishment of new lines, and then to give information on timetabling. The posters were similar to those made earlier by the stagecoach companies and were intended to be informative rather than persuasive or artistic. Notices were aimed at people who already planned to travel, and their designs were crowded with text and difficult to read, complicated by a variety of different typefaces. The notices were functional, put together by printers using standard blocks, and setting out departure and arrival details and information about fares. While these often contained no images, many others featured woodcuts of generic engines or carriages.

Opposite: 'Dukeries Route', Lancashire Derbyshire & East Coast Railway, 1897. The route opened to passengers in 1897, although the planned extension to Sheffield (shown in the poster as a dotted line) was never completed beyond Beighton.

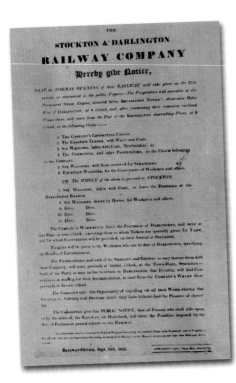

These were not necessarily accurate representations of the rolling stock used on the line being advertised; the same blocks were used for several different companies and were often many years out of date, but nonetheless they were a cheap and effective way to enliven the notices.

Further poster advertising was generated in the 1840s and 1850s when companies began running excursion trips in addition to their regular timetabled services. In 1841 Thomas Cook, founder of the famous travel agency, arranged his first excursion train with the Midland Railway, and such trains subsequently became very popular for days out at weekends and bank holidays. As well as running to seaside resorts and race meetings, special trains were put on for big events such as the Great Exhibition in 1851. Many poorer people could not normally afford rail travel, but reduced excursion rates allowed them to take day trips to special events. The economist Douglas Knoop, in *Outlines of Railway Economics* (1913), stated that 'The primary object of excursion fares is to induce people, who would otherwise not do so, to travel by rail, and to encourage those such as would travel a little to travel more.' Posters for these excursions followed the same style as the early handbills, presenting a jumble of information.

Notice of the opening of the Stockton & Darlington Railway Company, 19 September 1825.

This 1846 notice advertises a pleasure excursion on the Newcastle & Carlisle Railway, using standard printers' illustrations to catch the viewer's eye.

An 1845 poster for the London & Dover Railway shows how travel abroad had also become easier as railway companies opened up shipping links to the Continent. The London & Dover Railway (part of the South Eastern Railway Company) opened routes to Calais, Boulogne and Ostend via Dover and Folkestone in February 1844. Passengers travelled to the coast by rail before joining one of the regular steamer services across the Channel, and then journeyed on to Paris and other Continental destinations. Paris could then be reached from London in twenty-four hours, as opposed to several days in a horse-drawn coach.

The poster used engravings in a circular frame around the text to represent the speed and convenience of travel between London and Paris achieved with the new technology. It features the London Bridge railway terminus, a locomotive and carriages, the cliffs of Dover and the English Channel. This was a progression from the old stagecoach-style notices and introduced an element of design by using the text in a roundel with radiating spokes, and adding the pictorial component. Like other railway advertising of its day, it still aimed to convey its message predominantly through text rather than image, which was confined to the edges. As well as issuing poster advertising, the company published an illustrated guide to its services giving advice on various aspects of travel. This included key attractions and facilities of the towns served, train and steamer times and fares, and information on obtaining a passport.

Engravings illustrate the route from London to the Continent in an effort to convey how quick, easy and convenient the journey had become. c.1845.

Leisure, landscape and outdoor activities were early themes for railway advertising, and most posters showed scenic images of lakes, valleys and the countryside. Towards the end of the century, as competition between companies reached its peak, the railways began to increase the comfort of their services, as well as their speed. This was a necessary development because of the long distances being travelled and the additional time required for refreshment stops. Corridor trains with toilets allowed these stops to be cut, sleeping cars were introduced, and in 1879 the Great Northern Railway (GNR) introduced the first dining car for first-class passengers. These additional services were promoted in the hope of securing new passengers, although the style of the posters changed little.

Railway poster design developed slowly until the end of the century despite improvements in printing processes. In the 1870s technical advances in colour lithography brought about a new era of poster design in Europe, although this was slow to reach Britain and even slower to influence the way railway posters were produced. The lithographic process had been developed in 1798 by the Austrian Alois Senefelder, but it was not until Jules Chéret began producing colour lithographic posters in 1866 that its use in poster design began to be seen as a creative art form in its own right. Chéret, along with Henri de Toulouse-Lautrec and Alphonse Mucha, took inspiration from life and art, reflecting the most recent artistic movements and incorporating a new realism into their work. The British artists J & W Beggarstaff (James

Pryde and William Nicholson, also known as the Beggarstaff Brothers), Aubrey Beardsley and Dudley Hardy were influenced by the new use of bold flat composition employed by these continental artists, and they brought some of these exciting new design concepts to their own work.

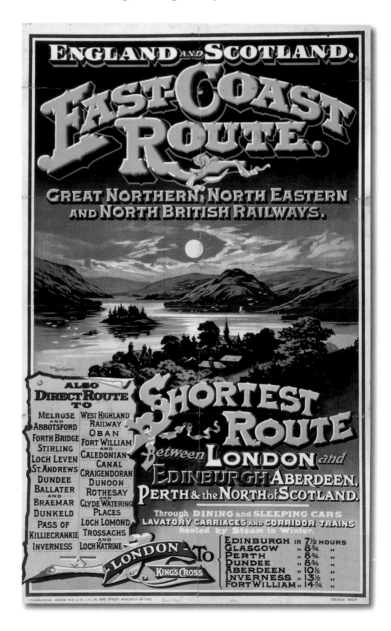

The Great Northern, North Eastern and North British railway companies used joint advertising (such as this 1895 example) to show that the East Coast route was the fastest and most comfortable.

However, the conservative nature of the railway companies, with their shareholders to please, as well as the high cost of printing in the 1890s, meant that these innovations in design did not filter through to their marketing strategies until the early years of the twentieth century. Although pictorial

The Great Western Railway's first known pictorial poster was issued in 1897 to advertise excursion trains to Ascot races. Although it uses only a single illustration, it is still complex and difficult to read.

MODERN ADVERTISING: A RAILWAY STATION IN 1874.

Above: 'Modern Advertising: A Railway Station in 1874'. This lithograph by Alfred Concanen shows the barrage of advertising in a nineteenth-century railway station.

Opposite top: This North Eastern Railway poster of 1898 shows the slow progress of poster design, with its mass of text and an array of typefaces.

Opposite bottom: Towards the end of the nineteenth century there was a move towards simpler composition and short captions, although the images still betray their conservative Victorian roots.

elements became more common, railway posters retained their busy composition and use of different sizes and styles of typeface. The Great Western Railway had appointed a clerk at the general manager's office in Paddington in about 1870 to deal with guidebooks and press advertising, and in 1886 it was among the first railway companies to create an advertising department.

To make it even harder for those trying to decipher all of this information, the posters were displayed alongside advertising for other products in a haphazard way and often on high walls, where they were even more difficult to see. From a distance it would have been hard to read all of the text and decipher the advertising message.

In 1900 W. Gunn Gwennet, a writer for the *Railway Magazine*, described the railway companies' output as 'antiquated puzzle posters'. Gwennet emphasised the importance of advertising for the railway companies but suggested that their efforts were wasted on such old-fashioned designs. In contrast to the work of the Beggarstaffs and innovations in Europe, it is easy to see railway posters as outdated. In posters of the later 1890s pictorial elements became more common, often with a few different scenes placed in vignettes over a background image and surrounded by text. These are, arguably, no easier for the viewer to decipher than the letterpress notices of a few years earlier.

The development from notices to 'antiquated puzzle posters' in the time before 1900 was the first step towards the pictorial railway poster that we recognise in the twenty-first century. Only after this period do we see the carefully chosen symbolism employed by twentieth-century artists and designers to attract passengers on to the railways. Through their

10

posters the railway companies presented certain lifestyle images to the public, much as modern advertisers do. Combined with the railways' capital investment in towns across Britain, their posters played a pivotal role in the growth of the tourist industry and built up what is now known as a 'brand' through which passengers could easily identify the companies. The posters projected an image of how the companies wanted to be seen, as fast, comfortable, affordable and convenient, and did not necessarily reflect the reality of rail travel for the average person. To begin with, the railways needed to tell people only what places they served, since there were very few alternative means of transport. However, as this changed they were forced to become more sophisticated in their approach. This led to the development of advertising departments and marketing strategies and, at the turn of the century, a change in style towards posters with bolder pictures and catchy slogans.

A NEW ERA IN POSTER DESIGN

B<small>Y</small> 1900 almost every town had a station and the rail network was more or less complete. Travelling for pleasure had become commonplace and there were now over one hundred railway companies vying for attention and trying to distinguish themselves from their rivals. For the next twenty years tourism continued to grow, encouraged by the railway companies' investment, and the role of advertising became increasingly important. Marketing departments were formed, illustrated holiday guides became popular, and the companies began adopting memorable slogans. The appointment in 1909 of Frank Pick as head of the Traffic, Development and Advertising Department of the Underground Electric Railways Company of London (UERL), later London Transport, also set an example to the main-line companies, bringing a high standard of modern art to the hoardings.

In the early years of the twentieth century it was normal practice for railway companies to use printing agencies to source images for their poster advertising. The subjects were much as they had been in the previous century, focusing on coastal and rural holidays, walking, golf and other outdoor activities, and freight, but the companies were beginning to see the value of poster advertising, and slowly a small number of artists were becoming known for their work and beginning to stand out.

At the same time, a debate was going on about the advertisement of rail services on hoardings, with articles in the railway press discussing the importance of advertising. The *Railway and Travel Monthly* thought that text-based notices were best as they could be understood instantly, and the *Railway Times* was sceptical about the need to advertise public holiday traffic at all since it saw it as risky, expensive and dependent on the British weather. The *Railway Magazine*, on the other hand, stressed the need not only for advertising but also for advancement in poster design. It felt that a poster's message should be obvious through its picture, even to a passenger who did not wish to stop to read the text. Similarly, Gwennet's article for the *Railway Magazine* in 1900 argued that a poster should have one clear image that

Opposite: John Hassall was one of the most influential poster artists of his generation. His famous 'Jolly Fisherman' captured the public imagination for over a hundred years. The LNER reused the image in this 1926 poster.

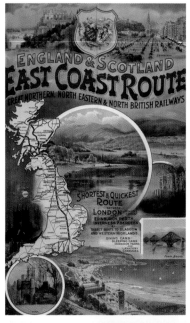

conveyed the company's message clearly to the customer and that the text should be subordinate to this. The image would grab the passer-by's attention and its thoughtful design would sell the product; in the case of the railways, planting the idea of travel into customers' minds and persuading them of their desire for a day trip, short break or even an overseas holiday.

Norman Wilkinson was an artist who speculatively submitted paintings in the hope of having them accepted by the railway companies for their advertising. He, too, was unimpressed by the design of pictorial posters that were being published at this time. He reiterated the sentiments of the *Railway Magazine*, describing them as 'an uninspired jumble of small views of resorts ... with a good deal of meaningless decoration...' and 'quite unintelligible at a distance'. In 1905 he produced a poster for the London & North Western Railway (LNWR) that stood out from many of its predecessors. The design for 'To Ireland' was submitted speculatively to the LNWR and Wilkinson took this opportunity to do something new, depicting a simple view of a steamer in the Irish Sea. The directors of the company were not keen on his realistic depiction, however, thinking that the ship should be more prominent, and it was only through the efforts of the General Manager, Sir Frank Rea, that Wilkinson's design was used. In contrast to the 'unintelligible' posters that had come before, Wilkinson's poster used a simple, bold design and caused something of a stir in the press. In this poster the image told the story; the customer was not required to stop and read the poster as he passed but could quickly and easily see that on

Above: 'East Coast Route', c. 1900, jointly issued by the Great Northern, North Eastern and North British Railways. Even after 1900 posters were still complicated affairs combining numerous images, maps and information.

Right: 'Queen's Hotel, Penzance', Great Western Railway, with Alec Fraser's distinctive bubble writing, 1908.

the LNWR one could travel to Ireland on a modern steamer, enjoying a pleasant, calm crossing of the Irish Sea. Its symbolic pictorial content was felt to be superior to the explicit narrative of posters such as those for the East Coast route. Wilkinson had come down firmly in support of greater simplicity and clarity in both the image and composition of posters.

In the midst of this debate new principles of advertising were emerging and many companies began to create dedicated marketing departments and publicity strategies. In 1907 the Great Western Railway

This poster issued by the London Brighton & South Coast Railway and the Chemins de Fer de l'Ouest in 1907 uses an eyecatching image of three Scottish pipers to advertise their London–Paris route.

Keeping the text to a minimum, in 1905 Norman Wilkinson painted a calm Irish Sea with a small ship in the distance, which he intended to represent accurately the small tonnage of the steamer.

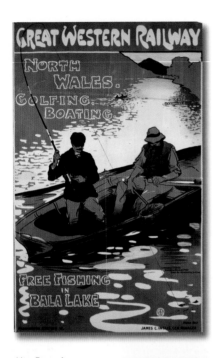

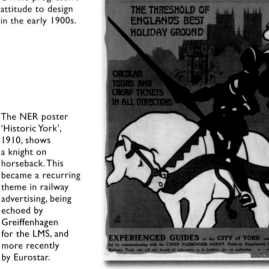

Alec Fraser's bold, simplified landscapes are easily recognisable and show the GWR's progressive attitude to design in the early 1900s.

The NER poster 'Historic York', 1910, shows a knight on horseback. This became a recurring theme in railway advertising, being echoed by Greiffenhagen for the LMS, and more recently by Eurostar.

(GWR) published an article called 'The Evolution of the Pictorial Poster' which explained to the reader how the railway poster had improved over the previous thirty years from crude lettering into a fine art. The GWR felt that its poster designs were leading the way in this development, publishing its best examples and discussing the 'mission' of the pictorial poster. The author said that the poster should 'tell a story at a glance' and 'excite interest'.

A favourite artist of the GWR was Alec Fraser. His posters for North Wales advertised a range of activities and showed how advertising was now being designed for people with specific interests. Outdoor activities were now much more open to those on middle and lower incomes and the railway companies continued to invest in golf courses, hotels and other facilities. With the arrival of the railways, the countryside had become more accessible than ever before and in the early years of the twentieth century outdoor activities became popular subjects for posters and illustrated guidebooks. Posters were designed with attractive scenes of recreational activities, emphasising the health benefits of fresh air and open countryside in order to persuade the viewer to visit the places depicted. The GWR's marketing campaigns also aimed to stimulate the imagination and it often formed its advertising around history, myth and legend.

The North Eastern Railway (NER) also saw the benefits of improving its poster design to include more artistic pictorial elements and saw how posters and advertising pamphlets could be used to appeal to a range of

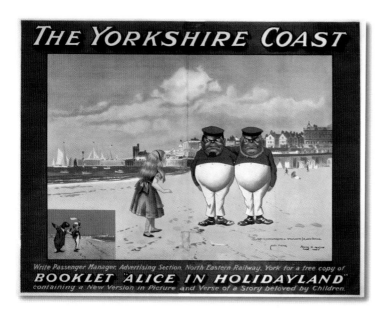

The NER poster 'The Yorkshire Coast – Alice in Holidayland' by Frank Mason, early 1900s.

The NER was a forward-looking company in terms of its advertising output. This 1907 poster for the Hull to Edinburgh service gives the train wings to emphasise its speed.

passengers of differing incomes. It also used historic themes, as in the poster 'Historic York', and parodied popular literature, producing a series of posters and guidebooks entitled 'Alice in Holidayland', advertising holidays on the Yorkshire coast. This campaign connected the elements of fantasy and escapism from the popular Lewis Carroll novel with holidays on the NER's route. The NER tried first of all to persuade passengers to travel to a specific destination and then to convince them to travel on its route rather than that of a rival company. Issuing holiday literature was important to this approach as it provided a whole package to excite and inspire the holidaymaker.

The Great Northern Railway (GNR) also issued some notable work, including, in 1908, one of the best-known railway posters ever produced. 'Skegness is SO Bracing' was designed by John Hassall and has been reproduced and parodied many times. The GNR took a novel approach to advertising a North Sea coastal resort, making a feature out of its windswept

position, with the word 'bracing' alluding to the traditional notion of a trip to the sea being good for the health, and the character of the jolly fisherman skipping along the beach representing a salt-of-the-earth regional 'type'. In the years that followed, these 'types' would become a common feature in railway posters, but in the Edwardian period it was unusual to see such a frivolous scene depicted. While recalling the health-giving benefits of a trip to the coast, the poster also betrays some of the brashness of the contemporary seaside resort, which had become hugely popular with the working classes seeking to escape the tedium of regular life.

In the first years of the twentieth century advertising gradually became more sophisticated. The introduction of targeted publicity campaigns and a conscious move to create a corporate image meant that poster design progressed. Companies were still advertising excursions and holidays just as they had done in the previous century, but now they were depicting happy families and outdoor activities as well as picturesque views. When they began to develop advertising and marketing departments, their aims moved from

'See Your Own Country First' from the GWR, 1908, compares Cornwall with Italy in order to encourage travel to the south-west of England. It is printed on tinplate.

providing information to the art of persuasion. In 1908 the GWR even compared Cornwall to Italy: 'There is a great similarity between Cornwall and Italy in shape, climate & natural beauties.' Companies also began to employ slogans to create a unified identity across their advertising, with the GWR becoming the 'Holiday Line', while the London, Brighton & South Coast Railway (LBSCR) was known as the 'Sunshine Line'. Supplementary material such as pamphlets, guides, postcards and carriage prints gave a unified feel to the publicity and provided passengers with the information they needed to plan their trip.

THE CORNISH RIVIERA

On the Sunny Shores of the Atlantic.

The GWR was so confident of its 'Cornish Riviera' slogan that in this 1914 poster it omitted the company name.

Named train services were introduced and the GWR had so much faith in the strength of its 'Cornish Riviera' branding that in one poster it even omitted the company name from all but the publication details.

Freight formed the major part of most companies' revenue, and as they modernised their facilities they advertised these services with posters and in the press. This was not aimed solely at industrial clients, however, as freight and shipping posters showed how the railways boosted the country's industry and economy, so improving their public image.

The main-line railway companies were gradually moving forward with their poster design, but none embraced the avant-garde as quickly or wholeheartedly as the UERL under the instruction of Frank Pick. Pick implemented high standards of advertising across the network, as well as setting aside specific areas for the display of posters. He commissioned a new typeface to be used throughout the company's advertising and signage, and introduced the now familiar Underground station logo. Pick wanted a unified and coherent approach to improve not only the marketing of the Underground railways, but the appearance of London and people's experience of it. He began commissioning some of Britain's best artists for his poster designs and aimed to bring art to the masses via the hoardings. His commissions included excellent examples of early twentieth-century design. The Underground's posters were thoroughly modern and contrasted with the staid and traditional-looking work produced by academic painters of the period, as well as some of the work of the main-line railway companies.

Slowly, however, they began to follow, although again there was disagreement as to what was most appropriate for poster design. Pick's supporters felt that modern works with bold line and colour were best, while others argued that a more painterly and academic style was appropriate.

The NER's poster map of 1909 emphasises the ideal location of the ports of the Tees estuary.

With the outbreak of war in August 1914 the Railway Executive Committee took control of Britain's railways to ensure smooth running of vital services for the military. Advertising on the hoardings was reduced to a minimum. Although some poster advertising continued during the war, much was removed and replaced by recruitment posters. Holiday travel was still advertised, however, with the emphasis shifting from overseas and seaside resorts to inland trips. In 1917 travel restrictions were enforced and fares were increased to discourage travel, although this had little effect. Rolls of honour were produced by the railway companies, at first detailing the percentage of their workforce who were fighting, and later commemorating those whose lives had been lost or who had been injured.

This period had seen the transition from complexity to eyecatching imagery. Posters were beginning to include pictures that not only showed an attractive image of the seafront or hotel at the end of the line but had become persuasive in their approach, selling the fantasy of 'holidayland'. It took some time before posters began to appear on the hoardings again after the war, and before the railways could get into their stride again amalgamation loomed.

First World War posters on a Lancashire & Yorkshire Railway noticeboard at a Liverpool station, 15 December 1914.

SEAFORD

Write for Illustrated
Guide to Chamber of
Commerce, Seaford.

SOUTHERN
RAILWAY

For Express Train Services,
fares, etc., apply at
S.R. Stations and Agencies

THE BIG FOUR

D URING THE WAR government control over the railways highlighted the efficiencies of companies working together, while maintaining healthy competition in some areas. Despite the successes of joint working, the war had left the railways run down, reinforcing the argument for amalgamation. On 1 January 1923 the many concerns making up the British railway network were grouped into four large companies, as established by the 1921 Railways Act. The new companies were the London Midland & Scottish Railway (LMS), the London & North Eastern Railway (LNER), the Southern Railway (SR) and the Great Western Railway (GWR).

Each of the new companies took a different approach to its advertising, with some experiencing teething problems. The SR took months to agree on its new structure, including that of its advertising departments, while the LMS had its own difficulties because of the geographical range of the network. The LNER, however, got off to a good start by appointing William Teasdale of the NER as advertising manager and launching a clear strategy for publicity. The GWR, the only company not to suffer significant upheaval, carried on much as it had before grouping.

There was a clear development in marketing strategy in Britain in the 1920s and 1930s as the railway companies became increasingly sophisticated in their publicity. The informative narrative posters with multiple images and large amounts of information of the late nineteenth century were replaced by those with one central picture and a short caption or title that was easier for the passer-by to read. These pictures were carefully produced to symbolise ideas of Englishness, history, pleasure, recreation, romance and style. Images of the countryside gave the impression of seclusion, fresh air and healthy recreation, while pictures of crowded beaches suggested the pleasure and spirited activity of the seaside resort. Posters depicted a world of fantasy and escape from the confines of daily modern life, and there was a new recognition that they needed not only to provide information but to persuade the viewer to travel. Above all, however, the posters produced in the twenty-five years of the Big Four were aspirational, allowing people of all classes to

Opposite:
Outdoor activities such as walking were very popular, as in this Southern Railway poster by Leslie Carr, 1930.

23

N°6 SEA SPORTS

EAST COAST JOYS
travel by L·N·E·R
TO THE DRIER SIDE OF BRITAIN

participate in a lifestyle of luxury and excitement.

The LNER led the field in inter-war railway advertising. Almost immediately upon amalgamation, the company issued an advertisement in the national press and on station hoardings stating: 'Our New Name. London and North Eastern Railway. Our Aim. To Serve You!' The LNER had arrived and it wasted no time in creating its own identity under the leadership and vision of Teasdale.

Teasdale was clear in his intention to devise a unified and coherent strategy for the LNER's advertising much as Pick had done for UERL, now London Transport. It was some time before the company could afford to unify the liveries of the rolling stock across the network and it needed to create visual continuity in other ways. Teasdale chose modern artists with commercial rather than academic styles, distinguishing the LNER from the other three companies. The first poster issued by the company in 1923 was 'York Minster' by Fred Taylor, an artist who had previously worked for the

Tom Purvis carefully used large areas of unprinted white space to model the sea in this series of six posters produced in 1931, which also show the influence of Japanese woodcuts.

Fred Taylor's poster beautifully illustrates the light and shadow of the interior of York Minster, capturing the history and grandeur of the Gothic architecture and the Five Sisters window.

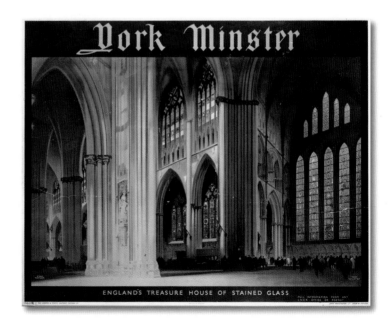

York Minster

ENGLAND'S TREASURE HOUSE OF STAINED GLASS

Midland Railway and UERL. The poster was well received by both the public and the press; the *Railway Gazette* reported on 16 March 1923 that it was 'one of the finest coloured posters ever issued in connection with railway publicity', and copies were sold at 10s 6d each.

The LNER continued its campaign with a series of lively posters, including in 1924 'Over the Nidd near Harrogate' by Frank Brangwyn, who, as the company was quick to point out, was the first Royal Academician (RA) to work for the railways. Later the LNER scored another first by commissioning work from Laura Knight, the first female RA.

Teasdale knew what he wanted from his publicity and the LNER soon gained a reputation for innovation. He was clear that each department must provide information regarding the places and services offered, but that the advertising department would decide upon the best course of action.

In 1924, Frank Brangwyn used the process of autolithography, working directly on to the lithographic stone, which gave an immediacy and freshness to the design for 'Over the Nidd near Harrogate'.

Dame Laura Knight had a particular interest in dance and circus subjects which is reflected in her brightly coloured, sculptural figures in 'The Yorkshire Coast', c. 1935.

The success of the LNER's strategies led to the company being at the forefront of marketing in Britain.

Teasdale and his successor, Cecil Dandridge, made use of memorable slogans such as 'Harwich for the Continent' and 'King's Cross for Scotland' in what was called 'reminder advertising'. These were designed to be catchy so that people would create automatic associations with principal routes, without the need to overcomplicate designs with text. They were complemented by posters for 'prestige services', such as the 'Silver Jubilee' train introduced in 1935.

In 1927 the LNER took the unusual decision to offer five of its most favoured artists contracts guaranteeing commissions for the next three years, with the agreement that they would not work for the other main-line railways. The 'big five', as Teasdale called them, were Tom Purvis, Frank Mason, Fred Taylor, Frank Newbould and Austin Cooper. The arrangement was renewed in 1929 by Dandridge, but their contracts were not renewed at the end of 1932 because of financial difficulties within the company. Nonetheless, all five continued to work for the LNER. as well as for the other companies.

The artists each had distinctive styles, with Mason producing marine images and Taylor architectural ones. Newbould's work was typified by his 'East Coast Types' series, which used a modern style in combination with an appealing traditional subject. Cooper and Purvis produced highly stylised designs influenced by the bold flattening of form and colour of twentieth-century painting, and Purvis's work also showed the influence of J & W Beggarstaff. Purvis produced some of the LNER's finest posters, such as 'East Coast Joys', a series of six posters that formed a single coastline when seen side by side. He used simplified shapes and skilfully employed white space and bright colours to give an impression of bright sunshine, and to capture the 'joy' of the

The strong lines of Frank Newbould's 'Silver Jubilee', 1935, emphasise the streamlined shape of the locomotive and the speed of the new express service between Newcastle and London.

title. The LNER's posters rarely advertised specific resorts and instead concentrated on regions; this allowed them a greater control over the advertising of these areas without the need to compromise their style by having to work with a town council.

Resort posters such as these were common in the inter-war period and showed a move away from the idea of resorts as healthy and invigorating and towards the fun and enjoyment of the seaside. People had started saving for annual holidays, and workers received paid leave and bank holidays. After the traumas of the First World War the seaside provided the ideal shared experience of fun, enjoyment and community. Each of Purvis's 'East Coast Joys' posters shows a group of people enjoying a different shared activity, selling the same basic beach holiday to different clienteles.

Both Purvis and Cooper were particularly concerned with the debates surrounding the rise of commercial art. Cooper argued against 'sentimental and academic presentation' in poster design. Writing about the poster's need to deliver a message, Cooper argued that the commercial artist's 'success must depend upon his ability to use his art persuasively, convincingly, in terms that his fellow men will understand'. This was something that Teasdale and Dandridge clearly agreed with, given their choice of artists and styles, and in 1923 they produced a display of posters at their King's Cross boardroom. The exhibition became a hugely successful annual event and in 1928 moved to the Burlington Galleries. This allowed further advertising away from the hoardings, and an opportunity to sell copies of the posters, which proved popular.

From 1928 Dandridge introduced standardised designs for the LNER's advertising, including the use of a standard company totem, or logo, and in 1929 the company followed the lead of UERL in adopting its own typeface for all of its publicity material – Gill Sans, designed by the artist Eric Gill.

'East Coast Types, No. 3 The Lobsterman', Frank Newbould, 1931. Fellow LNER poster artist Austin Cooper described Newbould's work as simplified realism with thoughtful composition and elimination of unnecessary detail.

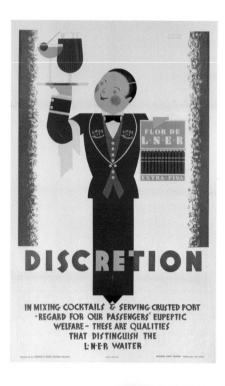

The GWR, having retained its original name since 1835, felt no great need to reassert its identity as the other companies did. It largely focused its efforts on a huge range of illustrated handbooks, regional holiday guides and other publications, such as *Holiday Haunts*. In 1924 the GWR named William Fraser publicity agent for the Publicity Department, but the poster output changed little. Although its posters by Alec Fraser had seemed fresh in the first years of the century, they became stale and backward-looking as the company carried on the outdated process of commissioning printers to produce them. As it had before the grouping, the GWR continued to compare parts of its network to the Mediterranean, such as in posters for 'The Cornish Riviera' by Louis Burleigh Bruhl.

The GWR felt that press advertisements were more helpful to the public than covering the hoardings with posters. In 1925 Mr D. Richards spoke to the GWR Lecture and Debating Society about the use of advertising and publicity. He

'Discretion', Austin Cooper, 1933. Cooper's highly modern style intergrated text and image to persuade the passenger of the superiority of the LNER's service.

The loose, painterly style of Louis Burleigh Bruhl's poster for 'The Cornish Riviera', c. 1929, gives it a warm and relaxed Mediterranean feel.

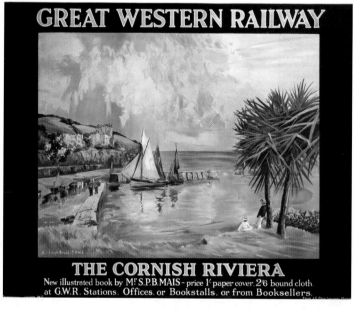

suggested that, although the poster was useful for the provision of information and the advertising of resorts and towns, press advertising was often more suitable. *The Railway Gazette* (13 February 1925) reported that 'Mr Richards expressed the opinion that one of the greatest failings of present day railway advertising is a too common use of the poster...', and, quoting Richards, 'I believe if the railways would tell their public in the press some of the things they endeavour to tell them by poster, they would achieve a much larger measure of real and useful publicity.'

On William Fraser's retirement in 1931 the GWR's advertising policy changed and it soon reached a peak with noteworthy commissions from artists such as Edward McKnight Kauffer. At the time McKnight Kauffer and other designers like him were applauded for introducing modernism to the public through well-designed posters displayed in public places. The GWR also followed the lead of the other three companies in using popular poster artists such as Newbould, Mason and Taylor. In 1939 the GWR published one of its most dramatic images, 'Speed to the West', by Charles Mayo, which moved away from landscape to

Edward McKnight Kauffer produced six posters of Cornwall and Devon, this one from 1933. Although not as determinedly modern as some of his earlier work for London Transport, the posters show signs of his earlier influence by the European avant-garde.

Charles 'Chas' Mayo's poster for 'Speed to the West', 1939, shows off the majesty of the GWR's 'King' class locomotives.

Early LMS posters often followed the styles of its constituent companies, such as this one, *c.* 1924, with the distinctive Midland Railway crimson border and slogan 'The Best Way'.

Bird's-eye views of coastal resorts like this one produced by Ronald Lampitt in 1946 were common.

focus on the locomotive and emphasise the theme of rail travel. It depicted the engine *King George VI*, a 'King' class locomotive – largest of the GWR fleet, and was produced with an accompanying book entitled *The 'King' of Railway Locomotives*.

The LMS carried on in the same manner as its constituent companies during its first year, with a style much like that of the Midland Railway, including the use of the Midland slogan 'The Best Way'. This is unsurprising as T. C. Jeffrey, formerly of the Midland Railway advertising department, was appointed Superintendent of Advertising and Publicity. At the end of 1923, however, the company felt a change was needed and asked the artist Norman Wilkinson how things could be improved. Wilkinson suggested that a series of posters by prominent Royal Academicians would do much for their public image. He was a great believer that art should play an important part in advertising, asserting that railway posters could 'interest and educate the public and relieve the tedium of what is still probably one of life's most depressing experiences – a wait in a British Railway Station'. In great contrast to the output of the LNER, the LMS agreed with his proposal and asked a number of RAs to produce poster designs. Frank Brangwyn, however, declined the offer as he was already working for the LNER, but the works of sixteen Royal Academicians, including George Clausen, Leonard Campbell Taylor, Frederick Cayley Robinson, William Orpen and Stanhope Forbes, along with Wilkinson's own designs, were issued in 1924, to mixed reviews.

The posters included all aspects of the LMS's network and activities, with numerous castles and views as well as the company's role serving industry. Although the series was intended to bring art out of the galleries and into the public domain, thereby elevating the railway poster into the realms of fine art, not all of the artists provided works in the academic style. Some artists translated their usual style and subject matter into something suitable for a poster. Frederick Cayley Robinson's design 'Cotton' was particularly successful as one of three in the series depicting 'British Industries'. The poster features a group of women weaving cotton, an unusual subject for a railway poster, however idealised the figures may seem. In the context of the railway poster, the anonymous women become part of British industry, elevated alongside 'Steel' and 'Coal', which were also featured in posters. They become part of the national workforce, served by the LMS.

Three more RAs, Sir David Murray, Sir David Young Cameron and Julius Olsson, all produced much more traditional works in keeping with the academic style of easel paintings. This reflected an inter-war love of the picturesque and again an interest in escaping the noise and industry of the city for the great outdoors. While the countryside was accessible to all, there was

Frederick Cayley Robinson's 'Cotton', 1924, is in keeping with the symbolist themes of idealisation and dreamy contemplation of his academic painting, while the sharp outline of his flattened figures shows the illustrative qualities of his work.

LMS **BRITISH INDUSTRIES**
COTTON
BY CAYLEY ROBINSON, A.R.A.

CAYLEY · ROBINSON

a distinct contrast between the traditional academic painting depicting rural scenes and the more exciting images of seaside resorts. Stanhope Forbes and George Clausen both worked in the realist genre and they translated this to

Julius Olsson's poster of 1924 sold an idea of peace and seclusion that could be found on a visit to Dunluce Castle. The light pouring out of the castle adds both romance and drama to the destination.

George Clausen's paintings often depicted rural labour; for his LMS commission in 1924 he translated this theme to an industrial scene showing workers silhouetted against LMS coal wagons and a mine.

fit with the modern subject of the railways. Clausen produced 'Coal', another of the 'British Industries' posters, while Forbes depicted 'The Permanent Way'. Both showed images of the workforce that provided a contrast to the usual resort and countryside posters.

'Carlisle', by Maurice Greiffenhagen RA, was the most popular poster of the series, selling in great numbers. It depicts a knight on horseback, suggesting the long history of the city. In the catalogue for the series, Sir Martin Conway wrote:

> The knight immediately suggests mediaeval romance … it [Carlisle] is rather an emblem suggesting geographically the entrance to a highland region of natural beauty, and historically an avenue of approach to great realms of glorious and romantic history. This is the artist's point of view, and these are the suggestions his picture will excite in minds suitably attuned.

The LMS aimed to form a distinct identity through this campaign by aligning themselves with what Norman Wilkinson described as 'all that is good and

'Carlisle' by Maurice Greiffenhagen, 1924, presented Carlisle as a city of romantic history and was hugely popular with the public.

LMS **CARLISLE**
THE GATEWAY TO SCOTLAND.
BY MAURICE GREIFFENHAGEN. R.A.

best in British Art'. The use of fine artists for commercial purposes was seen by some as a useful tool for improving public taste by taking academic art on to the hoardings. The original artworks for the LMS posters were also shown in galleries up and down the country and abroad, illustrating their wide appeal.

Initially, the Southern's poster production was disjointed as each of the constituent parts continued to issue its own material. In the year after grouping it began to come together, issuing scenic views of its region by artists such as Donald Maxwell with the poster 'The Lake District of Surrey'. At the same time, the Southern began a scheme of improvements and electrification across its network, which included the busiest commuter lines into London. This work caused delays and cancellations and a great deal of bad press and complaints, prompting the Southern to take action. Its General Manager, Sir Herbert Walker, appointed John Elliot as Head of Public Relations and Advertising and Elliot immediately launched campaigns to reverse the negative press, including 'The Truth about the Southern' and 'Telling the Public'.

A series of four 'Progress Posters' designed by T. D. Kerr was issued in 1925; they were titled 'Electrification', 'Steam', 'The Viaduct' and

Initially the Southern Railway's advertising looked dated in style, as with this view of Frensham Lakes by Donald Maxwell, 1924.

THE "LAKE DISTRICT" OF SURREY.

"Frensham Great Pond, set in one of the loveliest scenes in all England. Towards Hindhead are the wild and rugged hillocks known as the 'Devil's Jump.' Towards Frensham Little Pond and around it spreads as fine a bit of heather-covered moorland as one could wish to see, stretching untrammelled to the horizon and studded with pines." *From "Unknown Surrey."*

SOUTHERN RAILWAY
H.A.WALKER General Manager.

The "Lake District" of Surrey is within 40 miles of London and easily reached by convenient Train Services from Waterloo Station to Farnham. Another route is—via Haslemere Station.
    For full particulars of Train Services, Fares, etc., see the Company's Time Tables, or apply Publicity Department, Waterloo Station, S.E. 1.

'Rolling Stock', each detailing facts about the modernisation programme. Although dominated by text, these posters were modern in feel, with brightly coloured, stylised images. 'Electrification' depicted lines of electric units with the caption 'World's Greatest Suburban Electric', explaining: '700 miles of Southern Railway will be electrified by spring next year – 3 new sections open this summer – 3 electric for every steam train now running – total cost £8,000,000.'

The *Railway Gazette* reported on the success of the scheme on 7 January 1927:

> The result must be attributed, apart from the improved services themselves ... to the scheme of propaganda which has been consistently carried out since its initiation in 1924 ... Southern Railway passengers have accepted almost without a murmur inconveniences far more serious than those associated with conditions in 1924, due almost entirely to the spirit of friendship which has been cultivated.

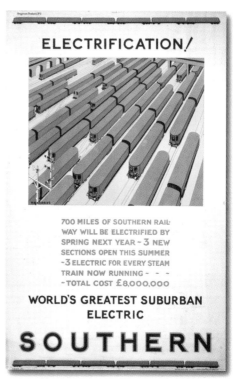

'Electrification' by T. D. Kerr, 1925, shows the beginnings of a modern style of poster advertising by the Southern Railway.

With a main route to Paris, the advertising of continental travel, including the 'Nord Express' and 'Golden Arrow' services, was a key element of the Southern's output. By 1926 Elliot felt that the company's poster advertising needed renewing and looked to the good examples of the LNER and UERL. In the late 1920s and 1930s the Southern issued a mixture of exciting modern posters. Of particular interest was a joint issue with the French Chemin de Fer du Nord by Cassandre (Adolphe Mouron) advertising the 'Nord Express'. In this poster Cassandre, a leading European poster designer, shows the influence of the Vorticists in his portrayal of the might of modern machinery. The Southern also issued a number of other posters in modern styles by Edmond Vaughan, Helen McKie and Shep (Charles Shepherd).

In contrast, one of the company's most successful posters was parodied by the LNER for its sentimentality; 'For Holidays I always go Southern 'cos it's the Sunshine Line!' depicts a small boy talking to an engine driver and was based on a picture taken by photographer Charles Brown. Such was its popularity that three thousand copies were printed, and the Southern launched a search to identify the little boy whose picture had been sent to the Publicity Department by Brown before the boy's family emigrated to the United States.

The strong diagonals of Cassandre's 1927 design symbolise the power and strength of the railway in this Vorticist-inspired poster for the Southern Railway and the French Chemin de Fer du Nord.

The poster was part of a wider campaign advertising the suitability of the south coast for holidays, featuring slogans such as 'The sun shines most on the Southern Coast' and 'South for Winter Sunshine'. 'Sunny South Sam' was introduced in 1930 as the friendly face of the Southern. He appeared on a range of publicity and a novelty song was even published. Meteorological Office records were quoted on posters to show that the south coast had the most sunshine.

The Southern was also keen to promote its routes to London and the opportunities for commuting, highlighting the proximity to London and

Far left: Although this 1925 Southern Railways poster was in no way modern in its design, it proved extremely popular, having being parordied time and again since its first publication.

Left: The LNER's poster 'Take Me by the Flying Scotsman' by A. R. Thomson, 1932, gives a modernist take on a Southern Railway favourite.

facilities such as breakfast cars. Passengers were kept up to date on the progress of electrification, with new publicity being issued when lines were due for completion. Posters echoed this, with a new Southern lightning bolt logo and text emphasising the speed and ease with which it was possible to

The friendly face of the Southern Railway, 'Sunny South Sam', featured in a range of posters, press advertisements and publications. This poster was published in 1939.

The GWR poster 'Paignton' by Charles 'Chas' Pears, 1938, is typical of the inter-war depiction of bathing beauties. The public were not necessarily put off by busy-looking beaches, as this showed that a place was worth visiting and fostered a sense of inclusion.

As well as rail and shipping, the railways also expanded into air services. The GWR's poster design had modernised significantly by the time this poster was issued in 1933.

As well as rail and shipping, the railways also expanded into air services. The GWR's poster design had modernised significantly by the time this poster was issued in 1933.

travel between London and the surrounding areas on prestige services such as the 'Brighton Belle' and 'Bournemouth Belle'.

While each company took a different approach to the style of its poster advertising, there were certain common features and recurring themes. Images of the landscape and seaside were hugely popular and geographical advertising was the most frequent among all companies. By the 1930s there was an awareness that this type of advertising, while promoting places very well, did not advertise the railway as a method of getting to the destination. With competition from road traffic increasing, the companies made efforts to place more emphasis on the train itself. The LNER produced posters that showed views through the frame of a carriage window to illustrate the superior comfort and ease of the train over the car, and in 1933 created the famous slogan 'It's quicker by rail'. Bathing beauties in swimsuits frequently appeared in resort advertising, which also featured women in fashionable hats and capes on the beaches and promenades. Despite this concentration on passenger traffic, more than half of the companies' revenue came from freight and other

THE DAY BEGINS

'The Day Begins' by Terence Cuneo, 1946, shows maintenance work to the 'Princess Coronation' class locomotive *City of Hereford* in preparation for the day ahead.

Work on the railways was a reserved occupation during the Second World War and the companies were proud of their contribution, as this 1945 poster by Reginald Mayes shows.

services. They advertised facilities including shipping, freight and air transport, and their workshops, docks and vessels also appeared on posters. Frank Mason produced posters showing the companies' ships, and Terence Cuneo became known for his industrial posters such as 'The Day Begins'.

Although advertising continued during the Second World War, it became more functional. Passengers were asked 'Is your journey really necessary?' and reminded 'Railway equipment is war equipment' and 'Food, shells and fuel must come first'. After the war, in 1946 Mason and Newbould produced patriotic posters of London without bomb damage. On the eve of nationalisation the SR commissioned two posters, 'Waterloo Station – War' and 'Waterloo Station – Peace' by Helen McKie, which celebrated the station's centenary and showed it station in both war and peacetime. By the time the posters were issued, however, the Southern had been subsumed into British Railways and the Big Four companies had become one.

HERNE BAY

ON THE KENT COAST

Express trains from London (Victoria) BRITISH RAILWAYS *..through trains from the Midlands*

FREE HOLIDAY GUIDE FROM DEPARTMENT R.P., COUNCIL OFFICES, HERNE BAY

NATIONALISATION

ON 1 January 1948 the LMS, GWR, LNER and Southern Railway were nationalised. They had already been working together successfully, under the Railway Executive, for nine years since the outbreak of the Second World War and had made heroic efforts transporting evacuees, troops, goods and munitions as well as regular passengers, but they had suffered from a lack of investment and maintenance throughout the period. This situation made it impossible for the railways to return to their inter-war structure, and so they were taken into state ownership, becoming British Railways. The British Transport Commission oversaw the running of all modes of British transport, also including ports, waterways and lorry haulage, in an attempt at unified working.

The newly nationalised railway was divided into six regions, broadly corresponding to the old Big Four company areas, with Scotland as a separate region and the LNER's lines divided into the Eastern and North Eastern regions. The other regions were the Western, London Midland, and Southern. Over the next few years British Railways began to assert its own identity through its branding, with new liveries, logos and station signage. Publicity for each of the areas was run separately, with poster advertising reflecting particular markets, just as it had been before nationalisation, while overarching British Railways campaigns, such as 'See Britain by Train', were also introduced. Poster design in this period saw a continuation of old styles, themes and traditional imagery as well as the introduction of some new design elements. Traditional painterly images continued alongside cartoon drawings. The careful and deliberate composition of the formal design styles of Purvis and Newbould in the inter-war period gave way to a much looser form of stylised illustration. While many new artists were introduced in the British Railways years, a number of Big Four artists also carried on working, including Newbould, Mason and Taylor.

Despite the austerity of the immediate post-war years, the leisure industry grew significantly in the 1950s. British Railways took advantage to promote the highlights of its regions, and its seaside posters brought design

Opposite: 'Herne Bay' by Bromfield, c. 1956, shows the use of humour for seaside advertising in the post-war era.

'Go by Train, Quick, Comfortable, Convenient' by John Ferguson for British Railways, 1952.

Traditional landscape views like this one by Sir Herbert Alker Tripp, c. 1950, remained popular after nationalisation, showing a continuity with railway advertising since the turn of the century.

up to date, adding joy and humour. The seaside resort was by far the most common poster subject in the early years of British Railways, reflecting a peak in resort visitor numbers in the 1950s and 1960s. Some of its posters favoured the conventional approach, although others were vastly different to the styles seen before the war. Humorous cartoon styles were particularly popular for seaside scenes, while the image of the upper-class spa town had finally gone. Families featured heavily in seaside advertising, but many were generic scenes that could be anywhere, with

buckets, spades and deckchairs representing the fun that could be had, rather than selling the features and facilities of a particular resort as in the past. These symbols reminded people of the enjoyment and relaxation that could be found at the coast. Where beaches were shown in full view they were usually packed with people. Recreation was part of a shared experience that everyone wanted to be a part of, and a busy beach showed that this was a good use of well-earned and precious leisure time. As well as children with buckets and spades, resorts were still depicted as appealing to the glamorous and young, with carefree bathing during the day and fashionable couples promenading at night.

Reginald Montague Lander's 1956 poster is typical of British Railways resort advertising. Deckchairs, sun hats and beach-balls alluded to the fun that could be had at the beach.

'Bridlington' by Tom Eckersley for the North Eastern Region shows cartoon personifications of a bucket and a smiling beach-ball in a sun hat. It has an element of humour that is present in much of the artist's work. Eckersley had been a prominent poster designer since the 1930s, known for the simplicity and economy of his work. He felt that the 'man in the street' would react to 'beauty, wit and imagination' and that this could be done both with persuasion to sell the product and with artistic validity. Eckersley produced a number of designs for seaside towns such as 'Mablethorpe' (Eastern Region), which again has the artist's trademark light touch that simplifies and eliminates all unnecessary elements to depict a child in the sand. Eckersley depicts only the head, shoulders and feet in a semi-abstract and characterful composition.

Eckersley worked for London Transport, Shell-Mex and the General Post Office, and was a key figure in the development of graphic design as a discipline, receiving an OBE in 1948. In the 1950s he began teaching at the

Tom Eckersley's 1955 poster for Bridlington is minimal in its composition. The resort's name is the only indication of location, but it is clear that this beach is family-friendly and ready for the enjoyment of beach-balls and sandcastles.

Women in bathing costumes were often used to illustrate the fun and excitement of the seaside, as in Merville's depiction of Weston-super-Mare, c. 1955.

London College of Printing, where the first undergraduate course in graphic design opened in 1954. The first generation of modern designers graduated in the late 1950s and 1960s. At last the commercial and graphic arts had achieved recognition as a discipline in their own right, separate from the fine arts.

In the 1950s and 1960s bathing beauties in skimpy costumes were used to advertise a great many resorts, just as in pre-war advertising. Paintings, cartoon illustrations, photographs and montage were all used for this purpose. The women were highly fashionable and showed the changing styles of the period. While many other posters of the 1950s and 1960s also showed the influence of modern design styles like that of Eckersley and of his contemporary Abram Games, not all artists could be said to be following any specific art or design movement. The academic fine-art precision of previous years had given way to a more informal style, with seaside posters in particular nodding towards popular culture.

Women in bathing costumes were also used for the Southern Region series 'Arrive Earlier by Train'. The series featured photographs of bikini-wearing young women superimposed on cartoon clock faces, grandfather clocks, egg-timers, and so on. This was part of a campaign to encourage people to take the train rather than travel by car. The car had provided competition for the railways in the 1930s, but during the war fuel rationing restricted driving. Despite efforts to reduce the numbers of people travelling throughout the war years, passenger traffic had increased by two-thirds. Fuel rationing ended in 1950 and private motoring revived to challenge British Railways. A number of slogans were used to persuade the traveller that the train was faster and more comfortable than being caught in a traffic jam.

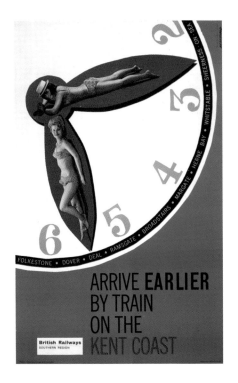

Passengers were shown relaxing, gazing out of a carriage window or reading, and comparisons were given to build a picture of a stressful driving environment.

While beach holidays predominated in advertising, sports ceased to be advertised as they had been before the war. Recreational activities such as golf and fishing, which had been an inherent part of Big Four advertising, were no longer seen on the hoardings. Instead there was a move towards excursions to watch spectator sports such as football and cricket; this was easy advertising for British Railways, being both cheap, using stock advertising images, and hugely popular.

At the same time, the contrary post-war themes of history and modernisation emerged. The Festival of Britain exhibition in 1951 celebrated traditional Britishness while looking to a future of recovery, rebuilding and redevelopment. Modernist architecture and design by some of the country's best artists was showcased in a vision of an ideal future. Abram Games designed the logo for the festival. As well as celebrating progress and opportunity, the festival looked back to the history of Britain, also marking the centenary of the 1851 Great Exhibition. This led to an interesting duality in both subject matter and style, which could be both rooted in the past and

Above left:
This 1963 poster by Bromfield was very literal in its imagery, designed to persuade the viewer that the coast could be reached more quickly by train.

Above right:
As in this poster from 1960, comparisons between rail and road often highlighted traffic jams and the stress of driving.

45

forward-looking, and this was also true of other British Railways advertising.

British Railways issued various series highlighting historic cities, monuments and themes, including the 'Our Heritage' series by the Southern Region. These posters showcased subjects such as castles, cricket, fishing, coaching inns and racing. Each contained a drawing of an historic figure with a smaller modern colour picture relevant to the subject, and some accompanying text to transport the viewer back into history. The 'Coaching Inns' poster in the series showed a sketch of a coachman and a picture of the George Inn at Southwark. The styles of these historic posters varied, as with the other subjects.

'York' by Edward Bawden played on the medieval character of the city. Bawden depicts a performance of the York Mystery Plays, which date from the fourteenth century, giving a sense of Englishness and continuity with the past. Bawden used lino cuts, which were popular with artists in the 1950s and 1960s as they were a cheap and versatile way of working. He was already well known for his illustrations in this medium and had done much work for London Transport before the war. His poster work for British Railways stands out as being unlike that of any other artist working for the railways, and his style is perfectly married to the subject matter.

Modernisation was badly needed after the war because of the poor state of the infrastructure and rolling stock. British Railways initially invested in steam locomotives, at first building to existing

Excursion trips were an easy win for British Railways, with stock poster designs being cheap and simple to produce. Bruce Roberts's edging for this excursion bill from 1951 recalls historic decorative borders in a highly modern, fashionable style and incorporates Abram Games's Festival of Britain logo.

The 'Our Heritage' series, c. 1950s contrasted historic characters in a simple line-drawn style with colourful painted scenes to represent the modern destination.

Big Four designs and from 1951 British Railways introduced the 'Standard' classes. Only ten years later, in 1955, British Railways published its Modernisation Plan, setting out the future for the network, including the end of steam and its replacement with diesel and electric fleets. Posters highlighted British Railways' work in these areas, just as the Southern Railway had emphasised the electrification of its network before nationalisation. Improvement was shown through images of modern rolling stock such as the diesel-electric Blue Pullmans, introduced in 1960. Terence Cuneo created a large number of images for the different regions relating to this modernisation. These included 'Progress', 'An Engine Is Wheeled' and 'Giants Refreshed'.

The landscape still featured heavily in British Railways poster advertising for all regions. The British countryside, historic cities and monuments were celebrated through posters. These had been common images within Big Four advertising and after the Second World War these themes of Britishness, tradition and history struck a chord of renewed patriotism and national pride. The countryside was depicted as a lush, idyllic place, and a healthy destination

Edward Bawden's 1954 poster for 'York' captures the historic architecture of St Mary's Abbey and the theatricality of the mystery plays.

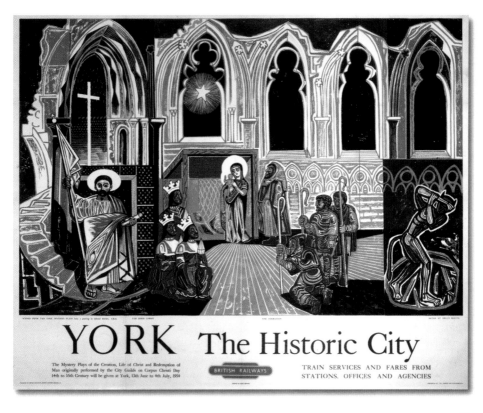

'Trains of Our Times', *c.* 1950, shows the progress of the modernisation programme, with a Class 5 4-6-0 steam locomotive, a twin diesel electric, and a suburban electric train.

for the family. Reginald Montague Lander's 'The English Lakes' for the London Midland Region showed a more modern and simplified style in design while retaining the traditional subject matter, although this was uncommon for

Terence Cuneo produced a large range of railway images, many of which were reproduced as posters. This 1957 example shows the construction of a 'Warship' class diesel hydraulic locomotive at British Railways' Swindon Works.

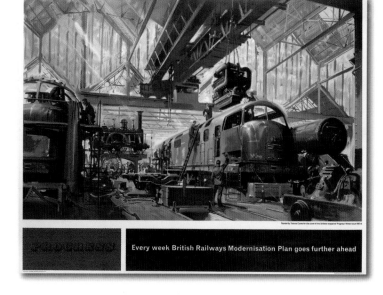

'Blue Pullman', 1960. Photographic printing technology had improved greatly after the war, allowing the time-consuming practice of lithography to be speeded up, and paving the way for the widespread use of photographs in poster advertising.

posters advertising landscapes; for the most part these posters were very conventional in style, with more modern designs reserved for less staid subject matter such as resort advertising. These images of the British countryside

London Midland Electrification, 1960. In the 1960s British Railways made great efforts to show how they were improving the network using slogans such as 'Getting on with the Job', which advertised the LMR electrification.

The stylised landscape of 'The English Lakes' (1955), with the block colour in the border and the simple title, gives a modern feel. The title emphasises the message of national pride at what England has to offer.

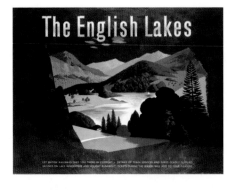

provided a reassuring continuity with the past after the upheaval of the war. Similarly, 'Yorkshire' by Gyrth Russell for the North Eastern Region showed an attractive and inviting view across the Dales. A farmhouse in the foreground showed the only activity, with a tractor and ducks in the yard. A ruined castle is visible in the distance to appeal to those seeking the romance of an historic ruin. Realistic and traditional landscapes were still hugely popular in the British Railways years across advertising for all regions. The progress of modernist design and integrated text that had been made in the inter-war period was forgotten in these designs.

'Yorkshire' by Gyrth Russell, 1948, gives a sentimental view of the countryside.

The Western Region in particular showed continuity with the pre-war days of the Big Four, using many of the GWR's former advertising themes and styles. Just as in the early days of rationalisation in the 1920s, the occasional 'rural type' crept into the scene, reflecting a recharged sense of

Above: GWR poster 'Picturesque Wales', 1901

British Railways' Western Region took inspiration from turn-of-the-century GWR posters depicting local 'types' in its poster for Barmouth. This 1962 version depicts a far more glamorous woman than its 1901 counterpart.

nationalism after the war. A poster by Henry Stringer for the Western Region echoes that of earlier GWR advertising, showing a woman in the traditional Welsh dress of red coat and tall black hat. She sits against a tree overlooking a bay with the caption 'Queen of the Cambrian Coast'.

The GWR had been very keen on myth in its advertising, with its *Cornish Riviera* and *Legend Land* publications exploiting long-standing local legends such as the Cornish mermaid of Zennor, which was appropriated for its own purposes. For the Western Region the mermaid motif reappears in a very modern cartoon guise in the Welsh poster 'Porthcawl', designed by Reginald Montague Lander. Produced in 1960, the poster shows a man holding hands with a mermaid; they gaze at each other, smiling. There are elements of the bathing beauty in the depiction of the mermaid, while adding the element of legend and quoting GWR history. 'Porthcawl has everything!', even beautiful mermaids, the stuff of fairy tales.

Early GWR literature often featured myth and legend; the BR Western Region modernised this idea with the use of cartoon imagery in this 1960 poster for Porthcawl.

Despite the volume of seaside posters produced in the British Railways years up to 1965, continental travel and sleeper services were also promoted. Overseas holidays had become cheaper and package holidays were taking off. British Railways' shipping services were heavily advertised, with artists such as Frank Mason showing off the latest ferries. B. Myers's 1958 poster 'The Continent via Harwich' shows one of its new ships in a semi-abstract modern style reminiscent of the landscape art of the Post-Impressionists. British Railways built a number of new ships in this period, reusing the names of past Big Four vessels such as the SS *Amsterdam*, which was advertised with impressive posters.

British Railways' advertising in the 1950s and 1960s focused on humorous and light-hearted imagery and its style was much less formal than it had been before the war. Seaside advertising outweighed most other subjects and the imagery reflected the informality of the resorts, contrasting with the formal design elements of the inter-war period. The Modernisation Plan was in place and posters showed new rolling stock and the progress of the electrification programme, but as a company British Railways was struggling and needed a dramatic rebranding that would distinguish it from its constituent companies and bring it up to date.

'The Continent via Harwich', 1958, was one of a series of posters by B. Myers, each in a bright semi-abstract style showing a Post-Impressionist influence that differentiates them from much of British Railways' poster advertising.

The shape
of travel to come

Takes off between Glasgow, Preston and London Euston

The most Advanced Passenger Train

This is the age of the train ⇄

BRITISH RAIL: UPDATING THE BRAND

BRITISH RAILWAYS underwent a period of significant change in the 1960s and 1970s. The Modernisation Plan was moving forward with main-line electrification, new technology and the end of steam, but these were difficult years, with a scaling back of the network, rolling stock and staff, to reduce huge deficits. British Railways needed to improve its image and encourage people back on to the railways. It was for this reason that in 1965 British Railways was rebranded as 'British Rail' (BR). This included the introduction of the double-arrow totem, designed by the Design Research Unit, a standardised railway alphabet and signage across the network, and standard liveries to create a complete and forward-looking corporate identity. The overriding theme was cohesion and modernisation, and care was taken that all aspects of BR's public image reflected this. The new image was unveiled at an exhibition at the Design Centre in London in 1965.

One of the highest-profile poster campaigns of the new era of British Rail was for the Inter-City service that was introduced across the network from the 1970s, of which the Blue Pullman was the 1960s forerunner. The Inter-City service utilised the new High Speed Train (HST), and prototype Advanced Passenger Trains (APT) were constructed; these innovations allowed higher speeds and greater passenger comfort than had been achieved before. Inter-City services were intended to provide high-speed links between the major cities, BR having realised that it could compete with road traffic only over longer distances, offering an alternative to the motorways. The advertisements focused on the speed of the journey and the fast times between city centres. This was emphasised by the imagery of the new trains, showing their streamlined shape. A predominant design element of these poster campaigns was the use of photography. It shows a modern approach, in keeping with BR's new image, and was able to showcase the stylish Inter-City rolling stock effectively. The posters look back to the advertising of prestigious-named services of the 1920s and 1930s. This modern look could not have been achieved with the relaxed cartoon style that had dominated the previous years; photography suited the sleek clean lines of the APT and HST

Opposite:
BR had high hopes for a new fleet of Inter-City Advanced Passenger Trains, as this 1981 poster, 'The Shape of Travel to Come', shows.

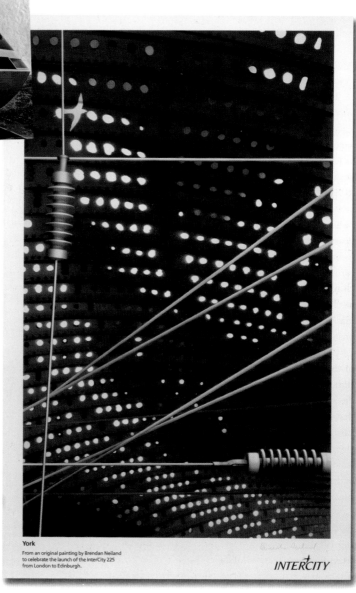

Inter-City 125
London-Bristol   London-South Wales
**Now: more trains
shorter journey times
still no extra cost to you**

and reflected the forward-looking nature of the rebranded corporate image. These posters all featured the double-arrow symbol, which quickly became one of the most recognisable logos in Britain. The campaign ran for many years and in 1988 was accompanied by a range of television advertisements, including the

'Inter-City 125', 1977. Photography was the ideal medium to show off the sleek lines of the new Inter-City 125 High Speed Trains. Images of the trains became much more popular in this period as BR showed off advances in technology.

Brendan Neiland's posters for the launch of the InterCity 225 look back to the great age of railway architecture, showcasing both the modern technology of the electrification scheme and historic station roofs. 1991.

York
From an original painting by Brendan Neiland
to celebrate the launch of the InterCity 225
from London to Edinburgh.

INTERCITY

popular 'Relax' by Saatchi and Saatchi. As railway technology progressed, publicity followed. Further posters were issued for sleeper services, and in 1991 Brendan Neiland's impressive series of six posters depicting architectural details of major stations marked the launch of the InterCity 225 on the East Coast main line.

In marked contrast to railway poster advertising of earlier years, BR placed particular emphasis on the product; the focus ceased to be on picturesque views of places to visit, but told the viewer why he or she should use the train rather than taking the car. Posters sold convenience and painted a picture of relaxed and carefree journeys, depicting a clear and visible contrast to the hassle of driving. In a period of mass car ownership, Motorail posters, like those for Inter-City, aimed to coax people out of their cars. Again, this saw a shift towards travel over long distances, the key feature being that the passenger could take his

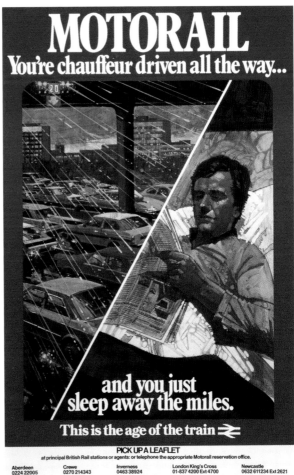

car by rail too. 'You're Chauffeur Driven All the Way...' depicts a man in a sleeping car reading his paper, while outside, in a contrasting scene, the rain is pouring down and traffic jams are backing up. The careful use of language and the word 'chauffeur' denotes an air of luxury and indicates that these posters were aimed at a customer who wanted to be well looked after.

The illustrative style of the 'Motorail' series gives a more informal feel than the photographic Inter-City posters, fitting in with the message of the campaign. 1982.

Notable by their absence are the seaside posters that were so abundant only a few years earlier. The seaside leisure industry, which had boomed in the 1950s, began to decline in the 1970s, largely as a result of competition from foreign package holidays, which had become cheap and convenient. The resorts that had emerged at the start of the century were beginning to look shabby from a lack of investment and could not compete with the draw of newer, fresher resorts abroad. High levels of car ownership enabled people to reach the seaside easily whenever they wanted a day out, and a week-long annual holiday at a resort such as Scarborough no longer held the same

Sealink posters took a variety of forms, but this simple design of 1975 gives the passenger a look inside the huge ferries for a glimpse of the facilities on offer.

attraction. Whereas in previous years resort advertising had been the major output, BR now moved its attention towards overseas travel. BR's Sealink ferry services took a range of approaches, including drawn illustration and photography, to cover a variety of themes and markets. The posters

The strong design element of the double arrow was used to frame photographs of different European destinations, including the Eiffel Tower in Paris and the Atomium in Brussels. 1981.

The 'Visit...' posters by Reginald Montague Lander had a distinctive flattened, airbrushed look that gave the series a cohesive feel. The 1979 castle has an angular look and minimal look that harks back to the designers of the 1930s.

advertised the sleeping facilities, food, times and cheap fares, as well as images of destination cities.

The advertising of historic sites continued during this period and is evidence of an enduring British nostalgia for the past. A series of 'Visit...' posters was issued, including 'Arundel Festival', 'Windsor Castle', 'Canterbury Cathedral', 'Hampton Court Palace' and 'Royal London'. These were designed by Reginald Montague Lander and all took the same format, in monotone with a sketch of the destination. By the 1970s it was becoming unusual for artists to be named, and Lander was a rare exception. BR also began using celebrity endorsement, with posters depicting the television personality Jimmy Savile, who advertised cheap fares, railcards and day return trips, all featuring the slogan 'This is the age of the train'. The use of celebrities reflected how alternative types of media such as television and glossy magazines had encouraged a new style of marketing based on popular culture. Celebrity endorsement did not stop with Jimmy Savile, and in 1979 the pop group Abba appeared in a poster encouraging passengers to 'Keep your station tidy'. Simple and functional posters like this, designed to encourage public co-operation, also became a feature on station hoardings, with other slogans asking passengers to 'Keep the train on time'.

As poster design increasingly had to compete with other mass media such as television, it began to lose its place at the forefront of advertising campaigns. The increased ease of photographic reproduction, and the economic benefits this brought, meant that avant-garde design such as had been seen in the heyday of the poster was no longer required. BR maintained a high standard of design for its core campaigns like that of the Inter-City brand, akin to the prestige posters of the Big Four, but much of its regular advertising became staid and functional. Nonetheless these posters belong to a far-reaching tradition of British design that evokes the joy of travel.

Throughout their history railway posters have paralleled the railway companies' development and growth, becoming ever more sophisticated in the art of persuasion. They provided information on the development of resorts, persuaded the viewer to visit newly accessible rural areas and encouraged continental travel. In the inter-war period the railway poster was a window into a world that could be aspired to; rambling and golfing, promenading and sailing – it was all achievable for the price of a train ticket. Avant-garde designs for streamlined locomotives and new technology reflected the modern art movements of the 1920s and 1930s, marrying style and content perfectly. From the early days of stock woodblock images, to the first steps towards coherent design, through the brief but prolific years of the Big Four and into nationalisation, the variety of styles and themes was astounding and will no doubt continue to capture people's imaginations for years to come.

Below left: The LMS and LNER had shown the bright lights of the big city in stunning paintings, but in the 1980s BR updated the theme with photography and celebrity endorsement.

Below: Clear, informative presentation was the order of the day by the end of the 1970s, as with this 'Keep Your Station Tidy' poster featuring Abba, from 1976.

FURTHER READING

Barnicoat, John. *Posters, A Concise History*. Thames & Hudson, 1972.

Bonavia, Michael Robert. *British Rail, The First 25 Years*. David & Charles, 1981.

Cole, Beverley. *Happy as a Sandboy*. HMSO, 1990.

Cole, Beverley, and Durack, Richard. *Railway Posters 1923–1947*. Laurence King, 1992.

Cooper, Austin. *Making a Poster*. The Studio, 1938.

Edelstein, Teri (editor). *Art for All, British Posters for Transport*. Yale University Press, 2010.

Happy Holidays, *The Golden Age of the Railway Poster*. Pavilion, 1987.

Hewitt, John. *The Commercial Art of Tom Purvis*. Manchester Metropolitan University Press, 1996.

Middleton, Allan. *It's Quicker By Rail, The History of LNER Advertising*. Tempus Publishing Ltd, 2002.

The Railway Poster in Britain (exhibition catalogue). National Railway Museum, 1997.

Rennie, Paul. *Modern British Posters, Art, Design and Communication*. Black Dog Publishing, 2010.

Shackleton, J. T. *The Golden Age of the Railway Poster*. New English Library, 1976.

Shaw, Gareth, and Williams, Allan (editors). *The Rise and Fall of British Coastal Resorts*. Pinter, 1997.

Sparrow, Walter Shaw. *Advertising and British Art, An Introduction to a Vast Subject*. John Lane, 1924.

Timmers, Margaret (editor). *The Power of the Poster*. V&A Publications, 1998.

Wigg, Julia. *Bon Voyage, Travel Posters of the Edwardian Era*. HMSO, 1996.

Wilkinson, Norman. *A Brush with Life*. Seeley Service & Co, 1969.

Wilson, Roger Burdett. *Go Great Western: A History of GWR Publicity*. David St John Thomas, 1987.

PERIODICALS

Railway Gazette
Railway Magazine
The Railway and Travel Monthly
Railway Times

PLACES TO VISIT

Didcot Railway Centre, Didcot, Oxfordshire OX11 7NJ.
   Telephone: 1235-817200. Website: www.didcotrailwaycentre.org.uk
London Transport Museum, Covent Garden Piazza, London WC2E 7BB.
   Telephone: 020 7379 6344. Website: www.ltmuseum.co.uk Archive
   by appointment.
National Railway Museum, Leeman Road, York YO26 4XJ.
   Telephone: 01904 686228. Website: www.nrm.org.uk
   Posters can be viewed by appointment in the Search Engine library and
   archive.
STEAM Museum of the Great Western Railway, Kemble Drive, Swindon SN2 2TA.
   Telephone: 01793 466637. Website:www.steam-museum.org.uk
Victoria and Albert Museum, Cromwell Road, London SW7 2RL.
   Telephone: 020 7942 2000. Website: www.vam.ac.uk Archive by
   appointment.

'Scotland by "The Night Scotsman"', London & North Eastern Railway, 1932 by Robert Bartlett.

INDEX